THE BIG BOOK OF
COLOR

Walter Foster Jr.

www.walterfoster.com
3 Wrigley, Suite A
Irvine, CA 92618

Illustrated by Lisa Martin and Damien Barlow
Step-by-step artwork by Diana Fisher
Written by Stephanie Meissner

Publisher: Rebecca J. Razo
Associate Publisher: Anne Landa
Creative Director: Shelley Baugh
Project Editor: Stephanie Meissner
Managing Editor: Karen Julian
Associate Editor: Jennifer Gaudet
Assistant Editor: Janessa Osle
Production Designers: Debbie Aiken, Amanda Tannen
Production Manager: Nicole Szawlowski
Production Coordinator: Lawrence Marquez

1 3 5 7 9 10 8 6 4 2

TABLE OF CONTENTS

GETTING STARTED

Welcome to *The Big Book of Color!* In this book you'll explore all the colors of the rainbow and learn how they work together. Discover how to combine two colors to make a new color, create different shades of your favorite colors, and use color to express feelings in your artwork. You'll even learn fun and fascinating facts about the colorful world around you!

Look for exercises throughout the book, where you can use crayons, colored pencils, or markers to color directly on the pages. There are also lots of step-by-step drawing projects that are perfect for practicing in your sketchbook.

There are tear-out pages at the back of the book to make into your own masterpieces. Each of these pages corresponds to a color project in the book, so you can practice what you've learned!

COLOR WHEEL

Fill in the color wheel, following the instructions on page 11.

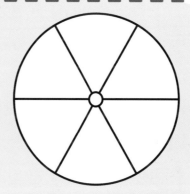

HAPPY MONSTER

Color in the happy monster with analogous colors, following the instructions on pages 18-21.

WARM & COOL COLORS

Color in these fun patterns with warm and cool colors following the instructions on pages 26-29.

TOOLS & MATERIALS

There are all kinds of tools for drawing and coloring!

Pencil, Sharpener & Eraser

Markers

Crayons

Colored Pencils

Paper

Paints &
Paintbrushes

Playing with color is extra fun with paint!
Experiment with mixing colors, and see how
many new colors you can make!

THE COLOR WHEEL

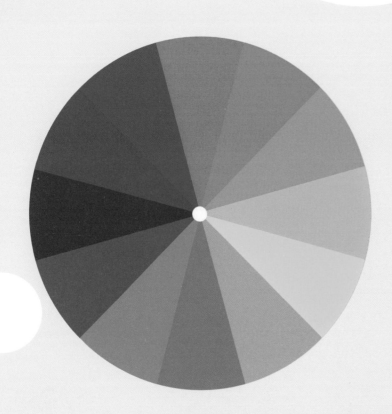

The **color wheel** shows us how colors relate to one another. Artists use the color wheel to understand the different colors and how to mix them.

There are three **primary** colors: **red, yellow, and blue.** These colors cannot be made by mixing other colors. But with these three colors, you can mix just about any other color you want!

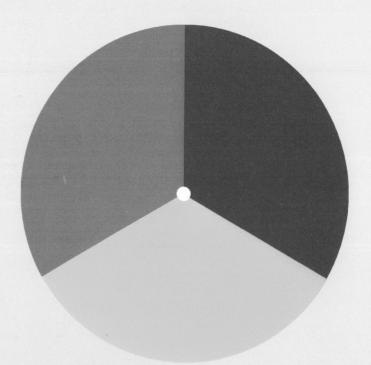

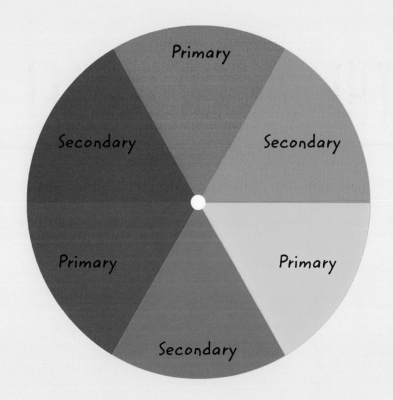

By mixing two primary colors,
you can create a **secondary** color!
Orange, green, and purple are secondary colors.

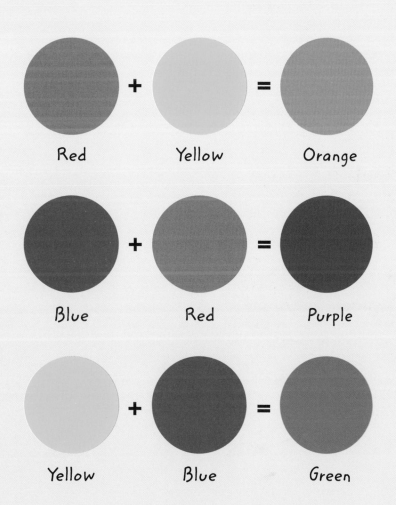

Red + Yellow = Orange

Blue + Red = Purple

Yellow + Blue = Green

When you mix a primary color with a secondary color, you create a **tertiary** color. Tertiary colors are yellow-orange, red-orange, red-purple, blue-purple, blue-green, and yellow-green.

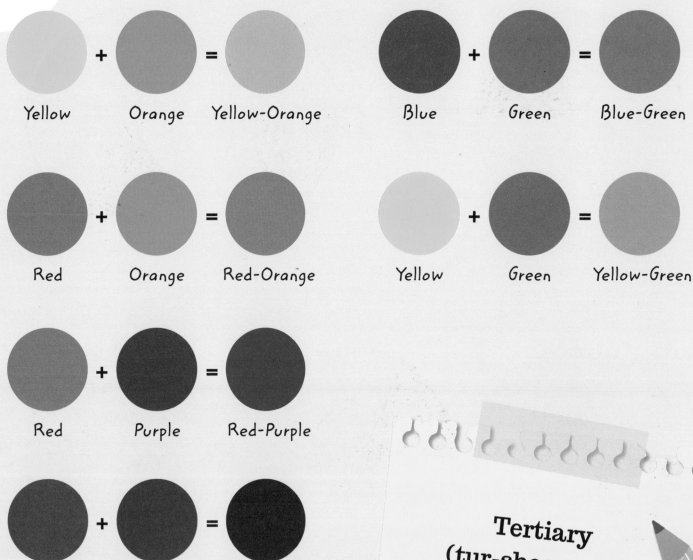

Yellow + Orange = Yellow-Orange

Blue + Green = Blue-Green

Red + Orange = Red-Orange

Yellow + Green = Yellow-Green

Red + Purple = Red-Purple

Blue + Purple = Blue-Purple

Tertiary (tur-shee-er-ee) means of third rank, importance, or value.

YOUR TURN!

Make your own color wheel to use while you create art.
Find the color wheel at the back of the book and tear it out.
Then fill it in with crayons, colored pencils, or markers.
You can also make your own color wheel with paints!

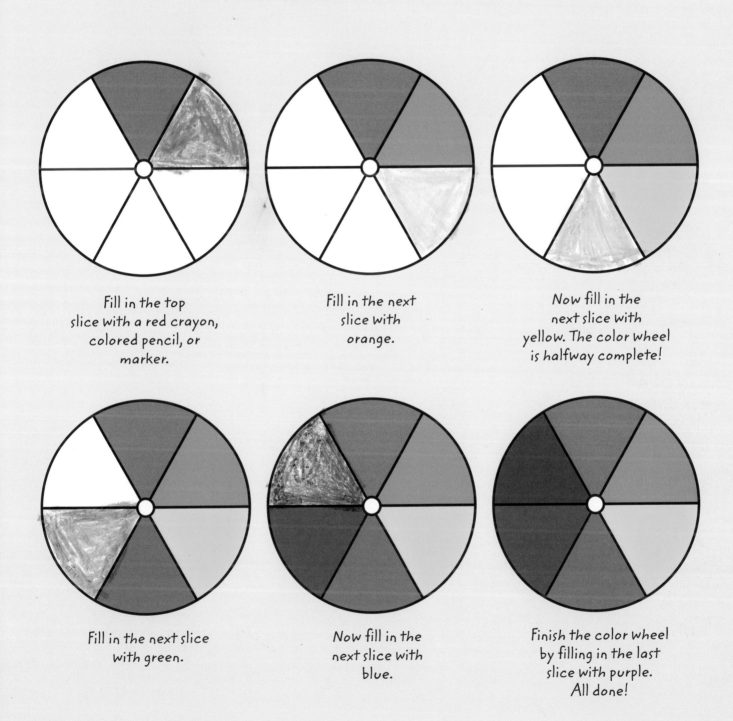

Fill in the top slice with a red crayon, colored pencil, or marker.

Fill in the next slice with orange.

Now fill in the next slice with yellow. The color wheel is halfway complete!

Fill in the next slice with green.

Now fill in the next slice with blue.

Finish the color wheel by filling in the last slice with purple. All done!

COMPLEMENTARY COLORS

Complementary colors sit on opposite sides of the color wheel. Complementary colors make each other look good when they are used together!

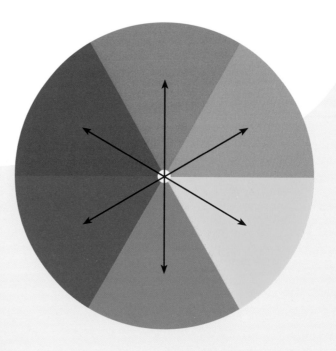

Look how vibrant the complementary yellow and purple squares are.

These squares are not as vibrant. That's because yellow and purple are complementary colors!

Complementary (kom-pluh-men-tuh-ree) colors make each other look brighter!

Yellow and purple are complementary colors.

Orange and blue are complementary colors.

Red and green are complementary colors.

COMPLEMENTARY COLORS IN NATURE

YOUR TURN!

Color these butterflies with complementary colors.
You can use crayons, colored pencils, or markers!
Look back to pages 12-13 if you need help remembering
which colors are complementary!

ANALOGOUS COLORS

Analogous colors sit next to each other on the **color wheel.** Analogous colors **harmonize** when used together.

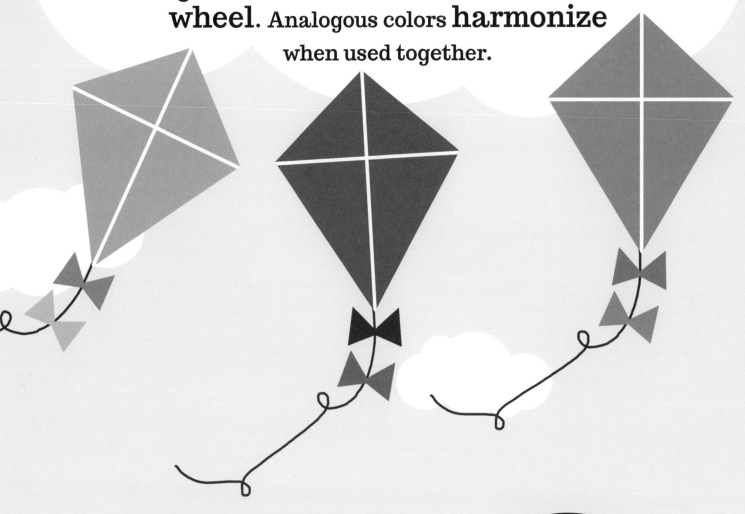

To make an analogous color scheme, pick any color on the color wheel as the **dominant**, or main, color. Then pick two or three colors on either side of that color.

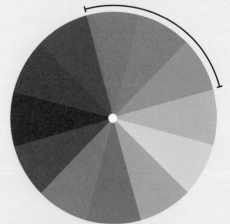

Red, red-orange, and orange are analogous colors.

Red, orange, and yellow are analogous colors.

Blue, green, and purple are analogous colors.

Red-purple, red, and orange are analogous colors.

Analogous (uh-nal-uh-guh-s) means "similar."

ANALOGOUS COLORS IN NATURE

YOUR TURN!

Find this happy monster on the tear-out sheet at the back of the book. Color the monster with analogous colors, using crayons, colored pencils, or markers! Look back to pages 18-19 if you need help remembering which colors are analogous!

Remember to pick one main color (such as green) first. Then pick two or three colors on either side of the main color on the color wheel (such as yellow-green and blue-green).

COLOR & VALUE

Value is the lightness or darkness of a color. Each color on the color wheel can be transformed into many different values, simply by adding **white**, **black**, or **gray**.

Here is the color purple in a range of values, from dark to light.

If you add **white** to one of the main colors on the color wheel, you create a **tint** of that color.
Tints are soft and light.

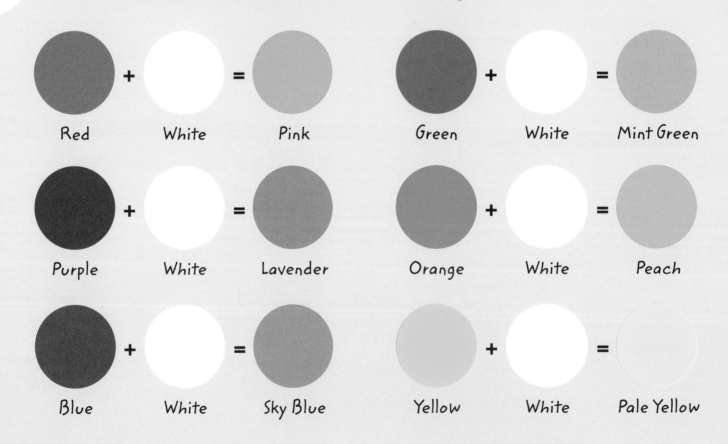

| Red | + | White | = | Pink | Green | + | White | = | Mint Green |

| Purple | + | White | = | Lavender | Orange | + | White | = | Peach |

| Blue | + | White | = | Sky Blue | Yellow | + | White | = | Pale Yellow |

If you add **black** to one of the main colors on the color wheel, you create a **shade** of that color. Shades are deep and powerful.

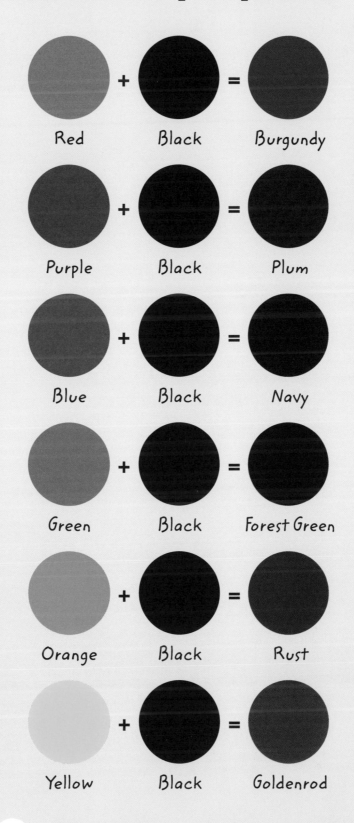

Red + Black = Burgundy

Purple + Black = Plum

Blue + Black = Navy

Green + Black = Forest Green

Orange + Black = Rust

Yellow + Black = Goldenrod

If you add **gray** (a combination of white and black) to one of the main colors on the color wheel, you create a **tone** of that color. Tones are muted and less intense.

Red + Gray = Salmon Pink

Green + Gray = Olive

Purple + Gray = Periwinkle

Orange + Gray = Marigold

Blue + Gray = Slate

Yellow + Gray = Taupe

You can use a lot or a little of white, black, or gray to create all kinds of **tints, shades,** and **tones**. Experiment with your paints to see how many colors you can create!

YOUR TURN!

Make your own value scale. It's easy!
Pick any color and choose five crayons, colored pencils, or markers in different values of that color. Then fill in the squares below from dark to light. Look back to page 22 if you need help!

MONOCHROMATIC COLORS

A color scheme that uses different values of just one color is called **monochromatic**.

Monochromatic (mon-uh-kroh-mat-ik) means something is one color.

These monsters are monochromatic. Each one is colored with different values of the same color—plus white for the eyes and teeth! How many values do you see in each monster?

WARM & COOL COLORS

Colors can be divided into **warm** and **cool**.

Warm colors include **red**, **orange**, and **yellow**.

Cool colors include **blue**, **green**, and **purple**.

Some cool colors are warmer than others.
And some warm colors are cooler than others!

Red is a warm color.
But red-purple is cooler than red-orange.

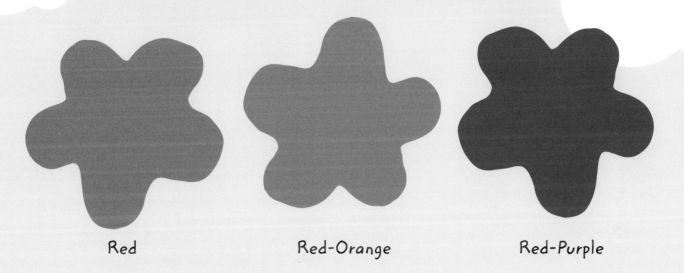

Red   Red-Orange   Red-Purple

Green is a cool color.
But yellow-green is warmer than blue-green.

Green   Blue-Green   Yellow-Green

Look for these symbols in the color sections on pages 32-119 to identify warm and cool colors.

Warm   Cool

Warm colors remind us of sunny days, fire, and heat.
Warm colors are active, and they seem to leap off the page!

Cool colors remind us of rainy days, water, ice, and the sky.
Cool colors have a calming effect, and they look clean and crisp!

YOUR TURN!

Find the two patterns below on the tear-out pages at the back of the book. Color one pattern with warm colors — lots of reds, yellows, and oranges! Color the second pattern with cool colors — lots of blues, greens, and purples!

COLOR MOOD

Did you know that certain colors make us feel certain ways? You can use color to express **mood** and **feeling** in your artwork!

Red
Energy • Power
Anger • Love

Blue
Peaceful • Loyal
Cold • Sad

Orange
Excitement • Movement
Brave • Happy

Yellow
Optimistic • Warm
Bright • Cheerful

Pink
Fun • Playful
Sweet • Friendly

Purple
Important • Artistic
Magical • Wise

Green
Calm • Fresh
Healthy • Relaxing

RED

Red is a **powerful** and **vibrant** color.

Red is a **primary** color.

The **complement** of red is **green**.

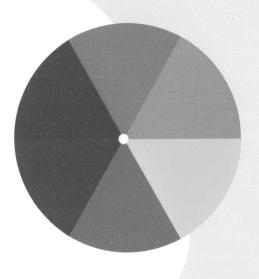

Red is a **warm** color.

THINGS THAT ARE RED

RED HUES

Auburn

Burgundy

Brick

Coral

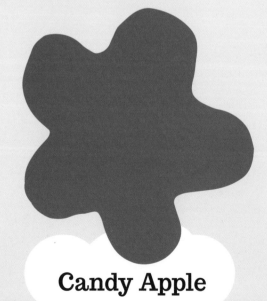

Candy Apple

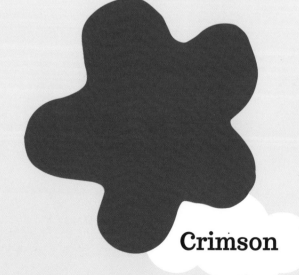

Crimson

Fire Hydrant

Maroon

Poppy

Rose

Ruby

Scarlet

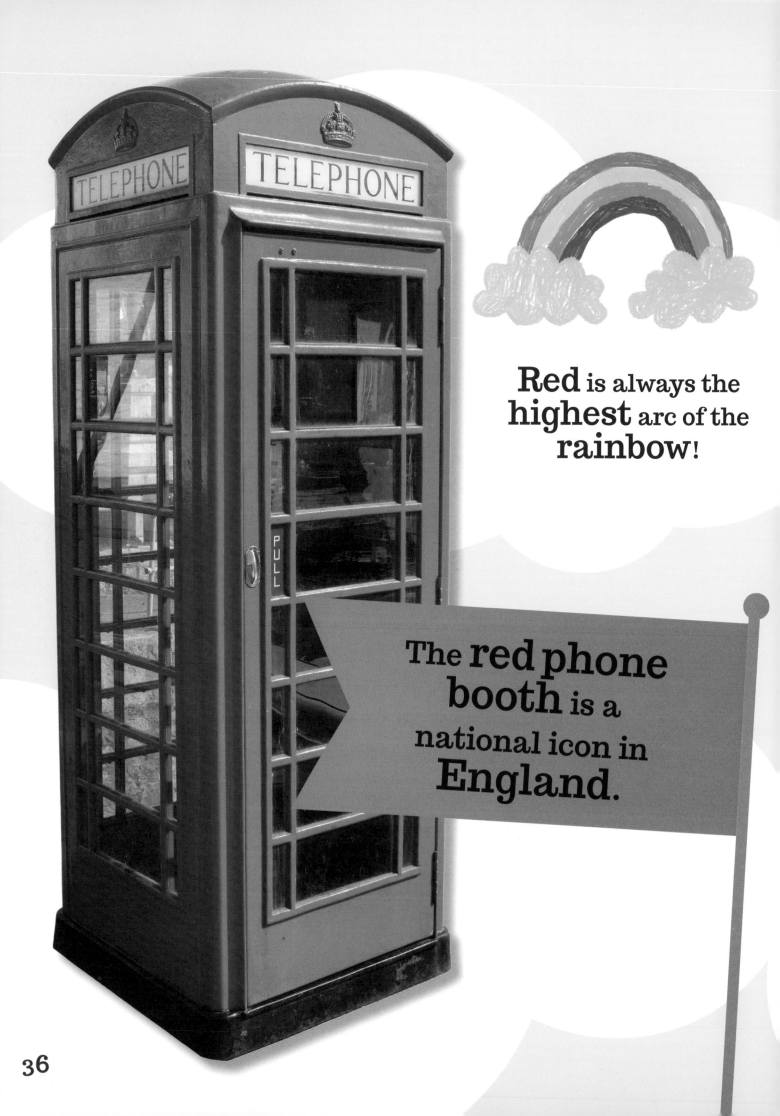

Red is always the **highest** arc of the **rainbow!**

The **red phone booth** is a national icon in **England**.

Not all **fire trucks** are **red**. Some are yellow, bright green, orange, or blue!

Only **male cardinals** have **red** feathers. Females are mostly tan with a bit of red on the wings or tail.

There are **26** known types of **chili peppers**, and they come in various shades of **red**, orange, yellow, and green.

Most **tomatoes** are **red**, but some varieties can be green, yellow, orange, pink, black, brown, white, or purple!

Red

is the international color for "stop."

STOP

Bees can't see the color **red**! Birds, butterflies, bats, and wind usually pollinate red flowers.

The biggest consumers of **ketchup** are kids, ages 6 to 12!

DRAW & COLOR THE HERMIT CRAB

A hermit **crab's** shell matches the color of the rocks, plants, or sand where it lives.

ORANGE

Orange is a **strong** and **energetic** color.

Orange is a
secondary color.

The **complement**
of orange is **blue**.

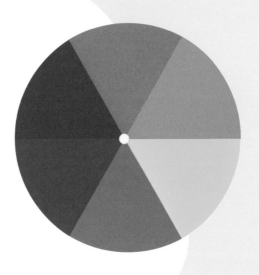

Orange is a
warm color.

THINGS THAT ARE ORANGE

ORANGE HUES

Apricot

Burnt Orange

Fiery Orange

Goldfish

Pumpkin

Carrot

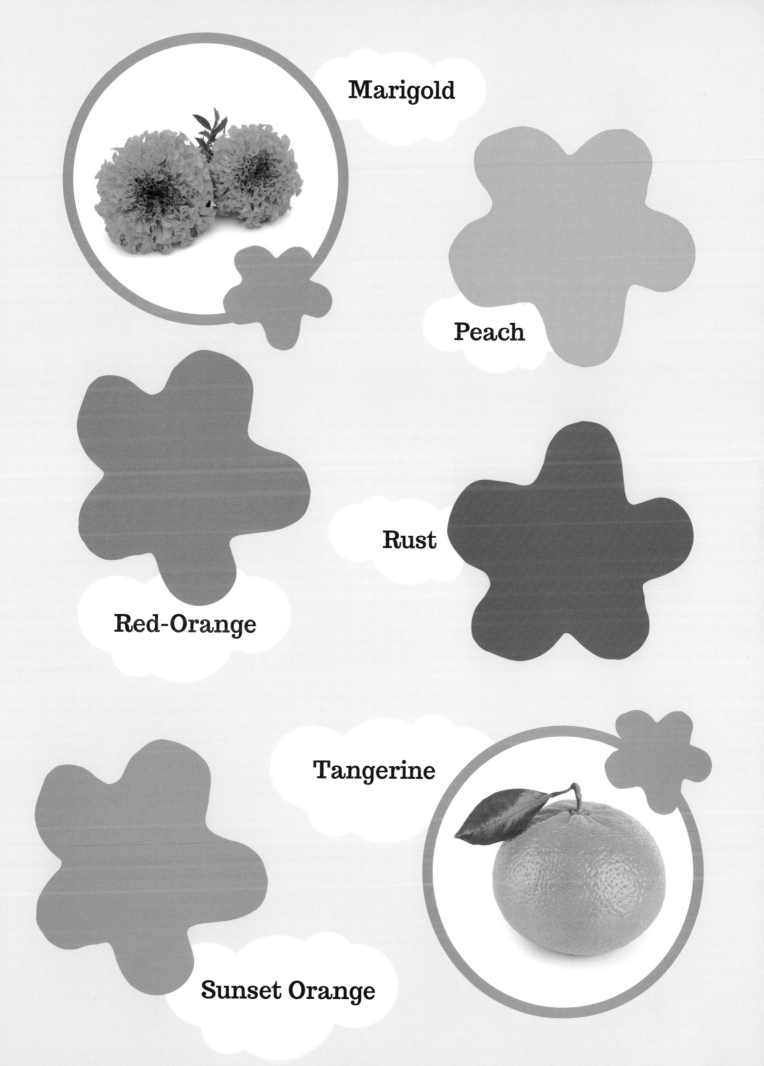

Marigold

Peach

Red-Orange

Rust

Tangerine

Sunset Orange

An average-sized **pumpkin** contains about 500 seeds!

Orange is the only color in the color wheel that got its name from a real object—the **fruit**!

Sweet potatoes are not actually potatoes! This bright **orange** root vegetable is part of the morning glory flower family.

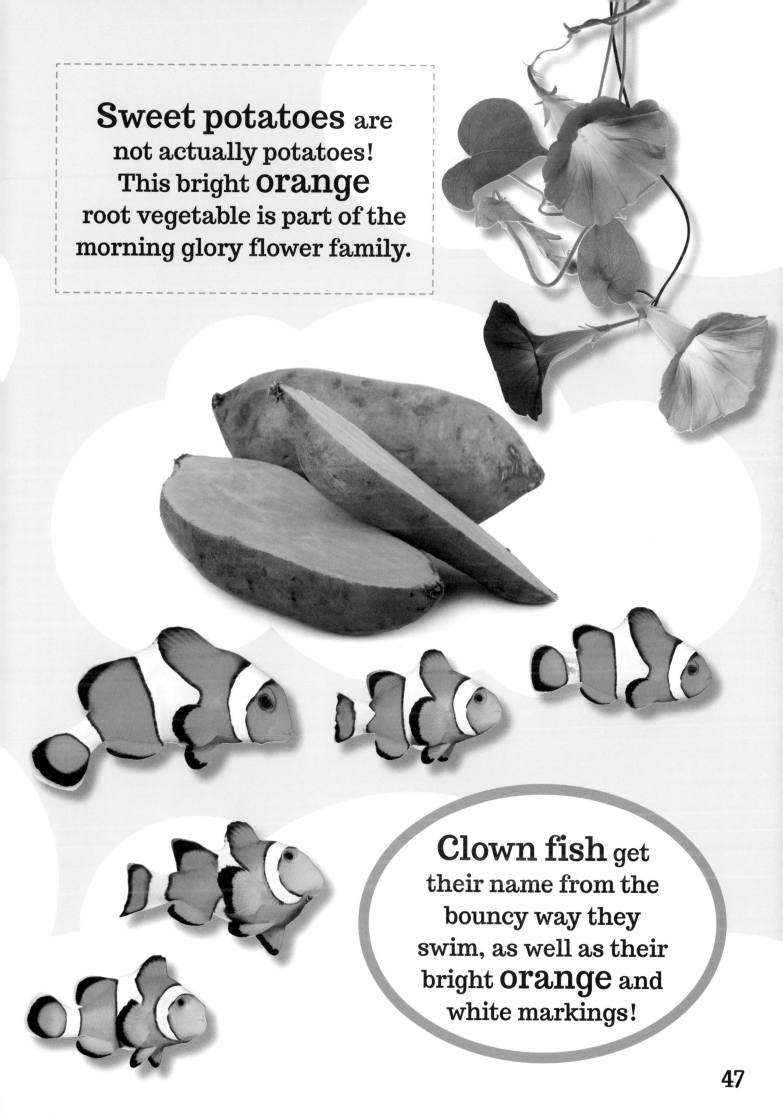

Clown fish get their name from the bouncy way they swim, as well as their bright **orange** and white markings!

A **monarch butterfly** starts out as a striped **caterpillar** before spinning a chrysalis for itself. After 10-15 days, the caterpillar emerges as a beautiful **orange** and black butterfly!

Carrots are usually **orange**, but some varieties are purple, red, white, or yellow!

DRAW & COLOR THE TIGER

A **tiger's** unique orange, black, and white striped **pattern** helps it blend in with its environment while hunting.

YELLOW

Yellow is a **bright** and **cheerful** color.

Yellow is a **primary** color.

The **complement** of yellow is **purple**.

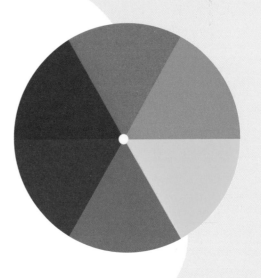

Yellow is a **warm** color.

THINGS THAT ARE YELLOW

SCHOOL BUS

YELLOW HUES

Banana

Canary

Goldenrod

Honey

Neon
Yellow

Lemon

Mustard

Many other **insects** mimic the yellow and black pattern of **yellow jacket wasps** to scare off predators!

Archaeologists think that **Native Americans** may have grown **sunflowers** as far back as **3000 B.C.**

53

The bright color of the **yellow tang** fades at nighttime to protect this **marine fish** from predators. When the fish wakes up, its **bright yellow color** returns!

Yellow is the color of **traffic signs** all over the world.

Humans can see all three primary colors (red, yellow, and blue), but **dogs** only see yellows and blues!

Mustard isn't naturally yellow — the seeds are brownish-gray! Mustard gets its **bright yellow** color from a spice called **turmeric**.

Baby wolves are born with blue eyes that turn yellow by the time the pups are **eight months** old!

Banana plants are not actually trees, but a type of **herb**!

DRAW & COLOR THE GIRAFFE

Each **giraffe** has a unique spotted pattern. **No** two are **exactly** alike!

BLUE

Blue is a **refreshing** and **calming** color.

Blue is a **primary** color.

The **complement** of blue is **orange**.

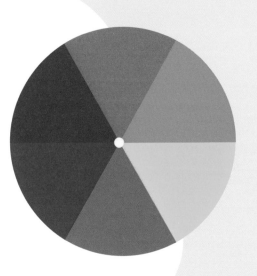

Blue is a **cool** color.

THINGS THAT ARE BLUE

BLUE HUES

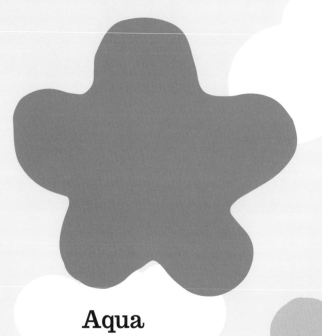

Aqua

Cornflower

Baby Blue

Denim Blue

Cobalt

Navy

Did you
know that
mosquitos
are **drawn**
to the
color blue?

Owls are the
only birds
that can see the
color blue!

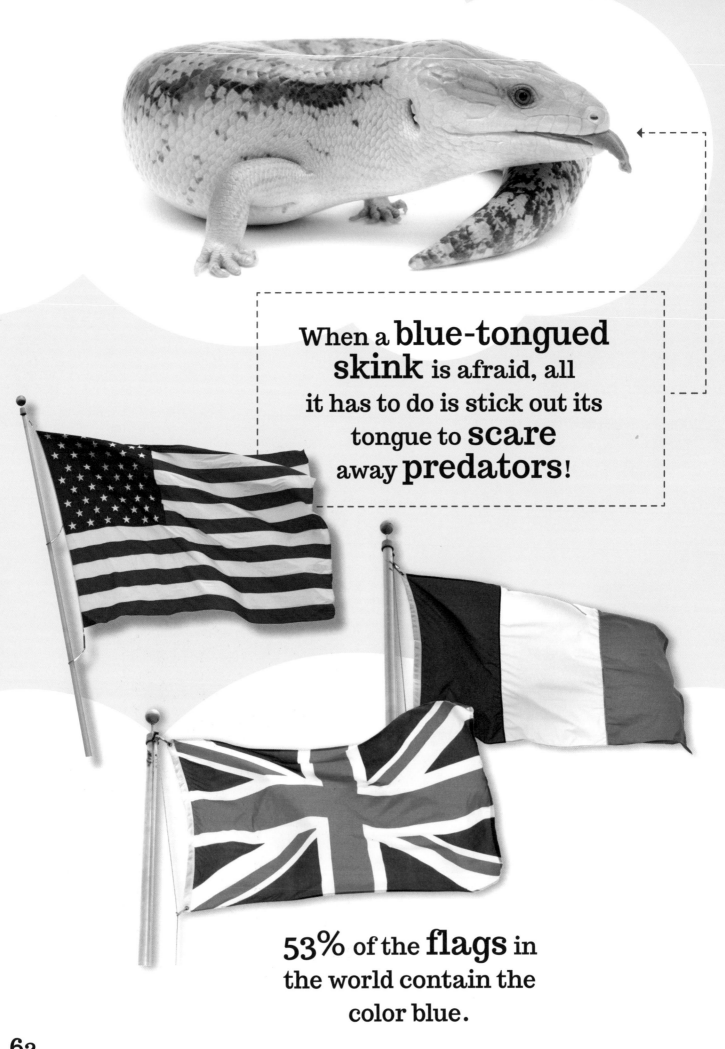

When a **blue-tongued skink** is afraid, all it has to do is stick out its tongue to **scare** away **predators**!

53% of the **flags** in the world contain the color blue.

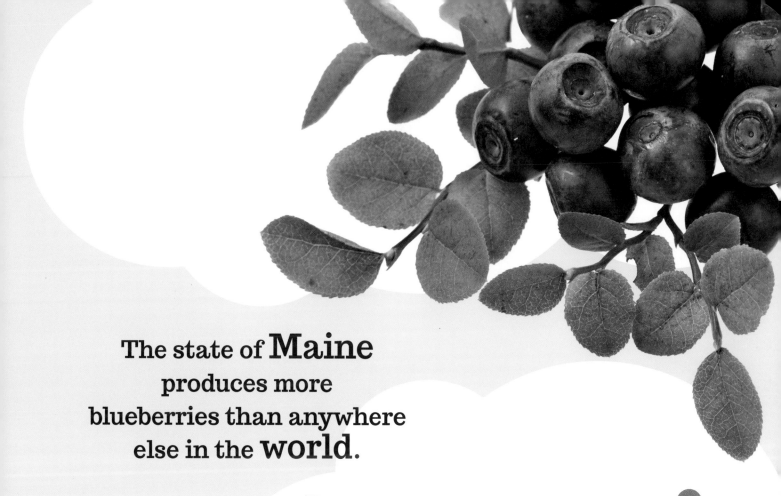

The state of **Maine** produces more blueberries than anywhere else in the **world**.

Blue is the most popular color for **toothbrushes!**

DRAW & COLOR THE WHALE

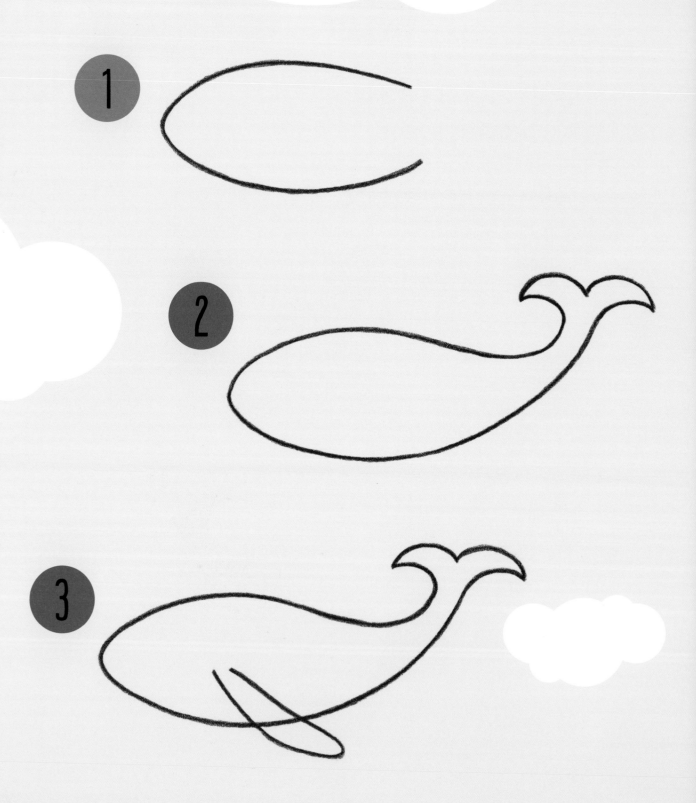

The **blue whale** is the **largest** living animal in the **world.**

PURPLE

Purple is a **vivid** and **relaxing** color.

Purple is a **secondary** color.

The **complement** of purple is **yellow**.

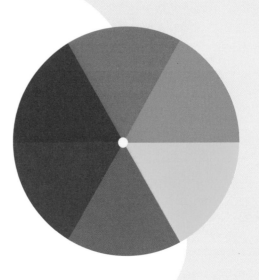

Purple is a **cool** color.

THINGS THAT ARE PURPLE

PURPLE HUES

Eggplant

Lilac

Grape

Plum

Lavender

Violet

Mulberry

Did you know that some **cauliflower** is purple? But under the **purple skin**, purple cauliflower is still white!

Lilacs come in a **variety** of colors, including white, pale yellow, red, and pink. But **purple lilacs** have the strongest **scent**.

There are more than **8,000** grape **varieties!**

It takes about **16 pounds** of grapes to make a gallon of **grape juice.**

In **ancient times**, it took about **12,000 sea snails** to produce enough purple dye for just one Roman **toga**!

The first **purple dyes** date back to **1900 B.C.** In those days, purple dye was **rare** and expensive. That's how purple became the color of **royalty and wealth**!

The **Chow Chow** is the only dog breed with a **purplish tongue** and lips!

Purple potatoes are popular in South America and are originally from **Peru** and **Bolivia**.

Eggplants aren't really vegetables. **They're berries!**

All **amethysts** are purple, but they can be different **shades,** including **lavender,** lilac, and **mauve.**

DRAW & COLOR THE STEGOSAURUS

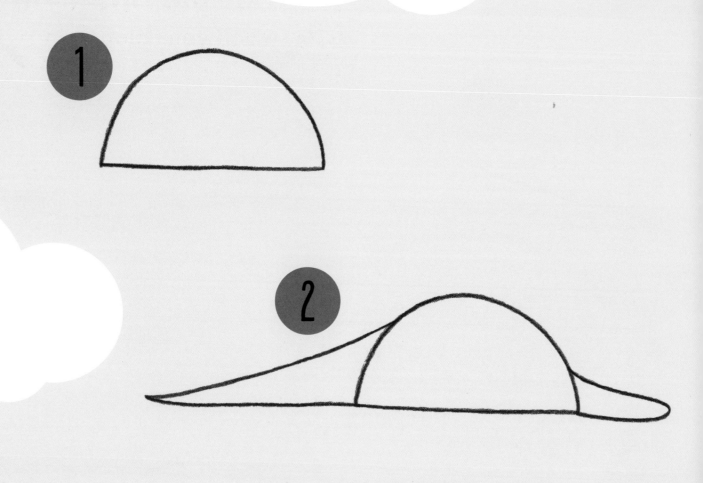

We don't know what color **dinosaurs** really were, which means you can use **your imagination** when you color them!

GREEN

Green is a **peaceful** and **refreshing** color.

Green is a **secondary** color.

The **complement** of green is **red**.

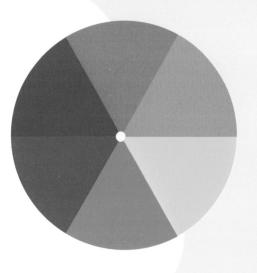

Green is a **cool** color.

THINGS THAT ARE GREEN

GREEN HUES

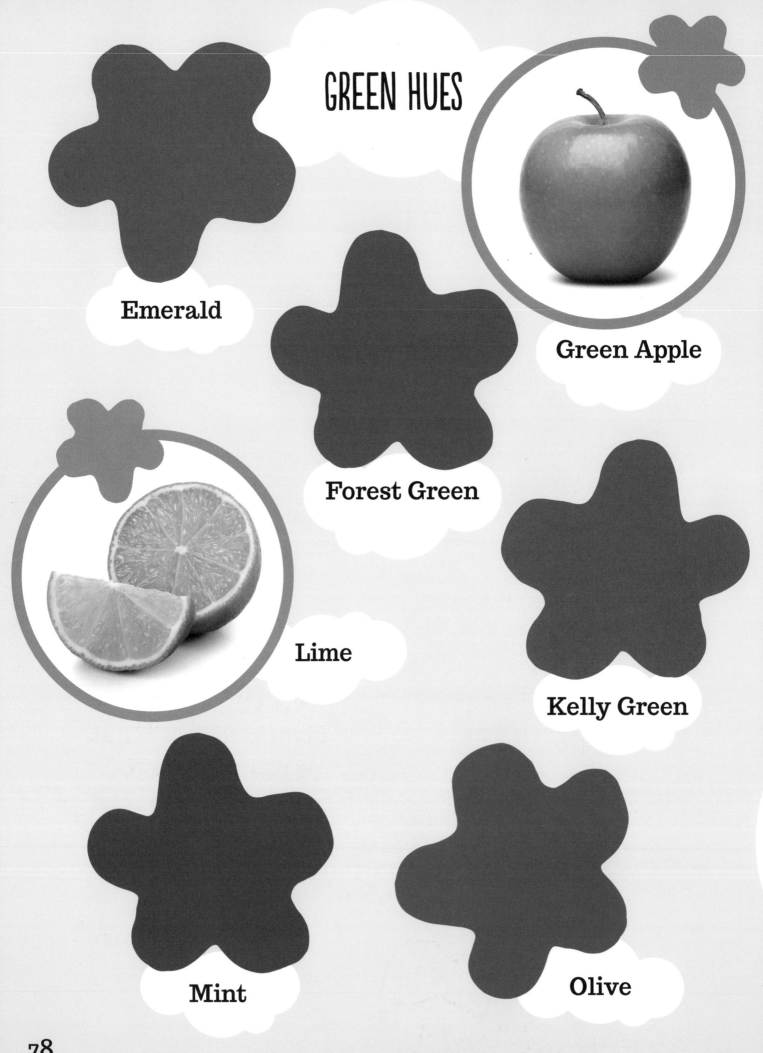

Emerald

Green Apple

Forest Green

Lime

Kelly Green

Mint

Olive

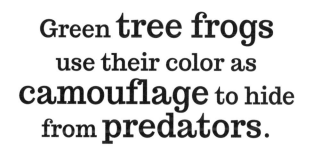

Green **tree frogs** use their color as **camouflage** to hide from **predators**.

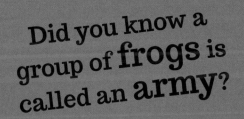

Did you know a group of **frogs** is called an **army**?

Green was **George Washington's** favorite color! What is your **favorite color**?

Artichokes are actually **flower buds** that haven't **bloomed** yet!

Green **sea turtles** are only **2 inches** long when they are born, but they grow up to **5 feet in length**!

Dark green vegetables have more **Vitamin C** than light green vegetables.

The Statue of Liberty in New York City has a **copper** exterior. Over time, copper reacts to oxygen and turns **light green**.

A **sloth's** hairy body has deep grooves where **algae** can grow during the rainy season, turning the sloth's **fur green** and helping it **camouflage** with its environment!

The **green basilisk** lizard has special feet that allow it to **run across water** to escape from danger. The lizard can sprint across the surface for **15 feet** or more!

DRAW & COLOR THE FROG

1

2

3

4

5

6

PINK

Pink is a **soft** and **comforting** color.

Pink is a **tint** of red.

Red plus **white** makes pink.

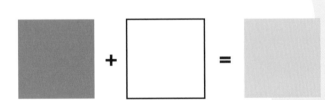

Pink is a **warm** color.

THINGS THAT ARE PINK

PINK HUES

Blush

Carnation

Bubblegum

Pink Lemonade

Fuchsia

Hot Pink

Magenta

Salmon

A **flamingo's** feathers are pink because of its diet! The **algae** and **shellfish** that a flamingo eats contain pink and orange **pigments**.

A professional **ballet** dancer can go through **100-120 pairs** of **ballet shoes** in one dance season!

Did you know that there are about **2 billion pigs** in the world?

What makes **pink lemonade** pink? Usually pink lemonade is **colored** with the **juice** of raspberries, cherries, grapes, or cranberries.

There is an island in the **Bahamas** with a **pink sand** beach!

Before there were **erasers**, people used moistened, balled-up **bread** to erase **pencil marks**!

Western Australia is home to several **pink lakes!** Scientists think the pink color comes from a dye created by **bacteria** that live in the **water**.

Cotton candy was invented by a **dentist** in **1897** and was originally called "Fairy Floss."

DRAW & COLOR THE JELLYFISH

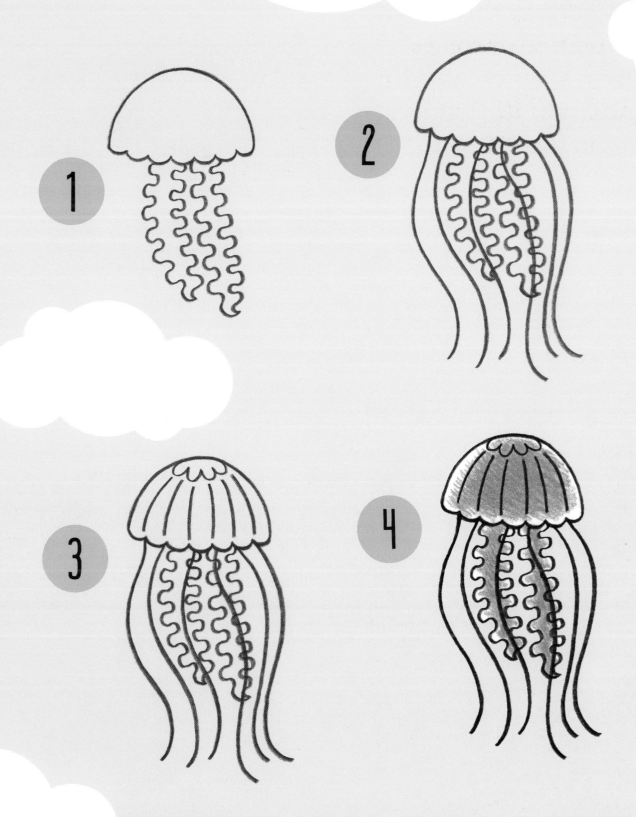

BROWN

Brown shades are usually very dark **oranges** or neutral **reds**.

Brown is **natural** and **simple**.

Brown is a **neutral** color.

You can mix **red** and **green** to make **brown**.

Try **adding** yellow, orange, blue, or purple to see what other **shades of brown** you can make!

THINGS THAT ARE BROWN

BROWN HUES

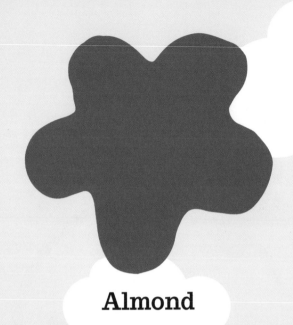

Almond

Bronze

Brown Sugar

Camel

Chocolate

Chestnut

Caramel

Cinnamon

Cocoa

Tan

Toast

Pinecones are actually the **flowers** of pine trees!

The world's **largest egg** was laid by **Harriet** the hen in 2010 and measured **9.1 inches** around!

Chickens with red **feathers** tend to lay brown eggs.

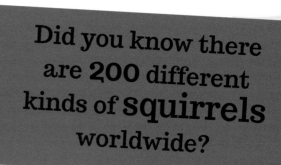

Did you know there are **200** different kinds of **squirrels** worldwide?

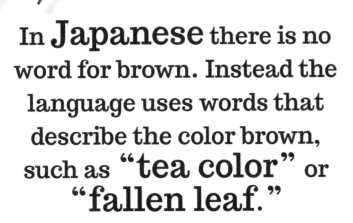

In **Japanese** there is no word for brown. Instead the language uses words that describe the color brown, such as **"tea color"** or **"fallen leaf."**

DRAW & COLOR THE QUAIL

GRAY

Gray is a color between **black** and **white**.

Gray is a **classic** color.

Gray is a **neutral** color.

You can mix **white** and **black** to make **gray**.

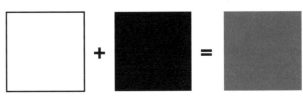

Use more **black** to make **dark** gray.

Use more **white** to make **light** gray.

THINGS THAT ARE GRAY

GRAY HUES

Charcoal

Stone

Silver

Pewter

Fog

Slate

The gray **tree frog** is named for its ability to **camouflage** itself by turning its **skin color** from gray to green.

Gray wolves have two layers of fur. The top layer **repels water** and dirt; the **thick undercoat** keeps the wolf warm.

Gray wolves range in color from white to black.

The **human eye** can see about **500 shades** of gray!

Gray is a **common color** for animals, birds, and fish because it provides a natural **camouflage** that allows them to **blend in** with their **surroundings**.

DRAW & COLOR THE ELEPHANT

WHITE

White contains an **equal balance** of all the colors in the **spectrum**.

White is **pure** and **clean**.

White is a **neutral** color.

White is **light**.

You can make **different shades** of white by adding **tiny** amounts of other **colors**!

THINGS THAT ARE WHITE

WHITE HUES

Bone

Pearl

Eggshell

Ivory

Cream

All **Dalmatians** are born white! The black spots develop as the **puppies** get **older**.

White tigers usually have **blue eyes**.

White tigers are very rare. The **gene** that makes them white is only found in **1** of every **10,000 tigers**!

Snow isn't really white — it's **clear** and **colorless** like rain! It only looks white because of the way **light** **reflects** off the snow **crystals.**

Cotton is grown in more than **100** **countries** around the world.

A **hen** must eat **four pounds** of chicken feed to make a **dozen eggs.**

A **COW** produces a little more than **6 gallons** of milk each day. That's **350,000 glasses** of milk in a cow's **lifetime**!

DRAW & COLOR THE POLAR BEAR

Polar bears are excellent **runners** and **swimmers**.

BLACK

Black is powerful and dark.

Black is a **neutral** color.

You can mix the three **primary** colors — red, yellow, and blue — to create **shades of black**.

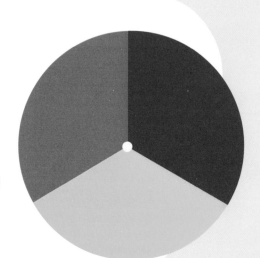

You can **add black** to another color to create a **shade** of that color.

THINGS THAT ARE BLACK

BLACK HUES

Coal

Black Licorice

Black Olive

Obsidian

Raven

114

In ancient England, **black sheep** weren't as valuable because their wool couldn't be dyed. But it was considered **lucky** to have one black sheep in a **flock**.

Giant pandas spend about 12 hours a day eating **bamboo!**

All **peppercorns** come from the same plant, but they can be **black**, red, green, or white depending on **how ripe they are.**

Underneath all that white fur, a **polar bear's** skin is **black!**

The color black **absorbs heat** and light. That's why wearing **black** clothes in the **summertime** makes you feel **hot!**

Most **road signs** are black and yellow because this color combination is the **easiest to see** and read.

Black is the **most common** hair color in the **world.**

Some people say that **black cats** are **bad luck**. But that's just a **myth**!

There are more than **1,000 species** of bats!

DRAW & COLOR THE RHINOCEROS BEETLE

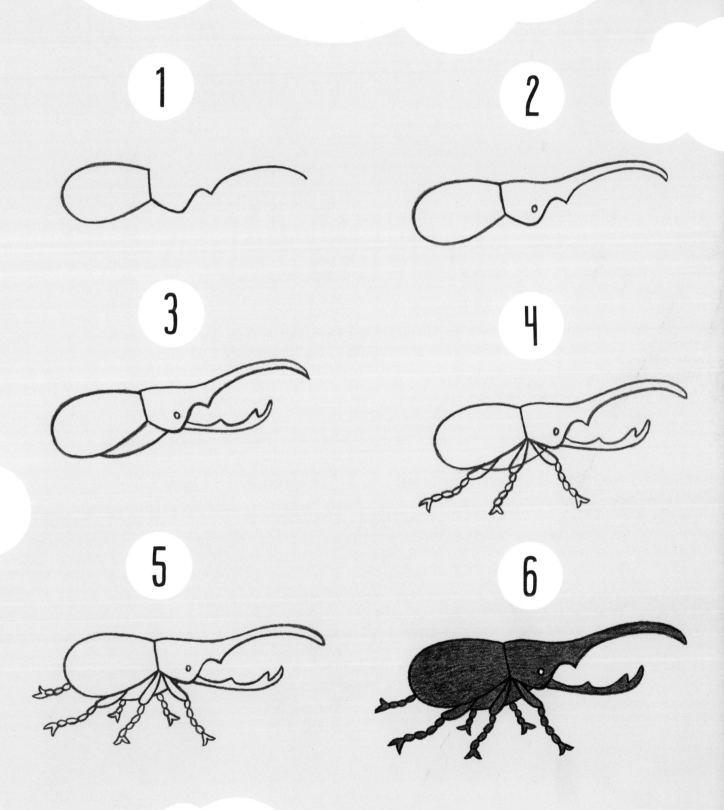

COLORING PAGES

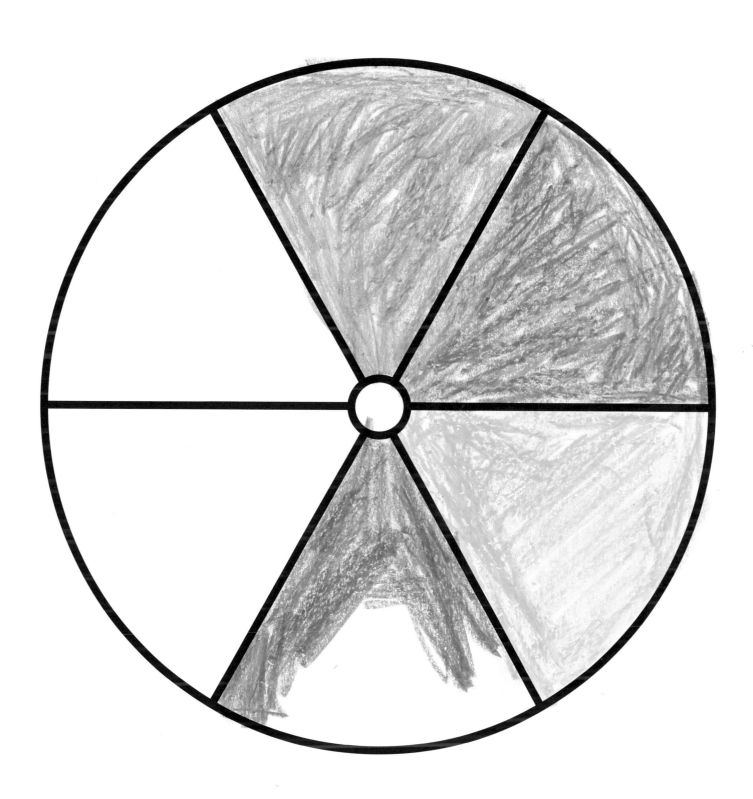